Music Genres

Latin Music

by Cynthia Argentine

FOCUS READERS®
BEACON

www.focusreaders.com

Focus Readers is distributed by North Star Editions:
sales@northstareditions.com | 888-417-0195

Produced for Focus Readers by Red Line Editorial.

Photographs ©: Thibaud Moritz/Abaca/Sipa USA/AP Images, cover, 1; Shutterstock Images, 4, 7, 8, 20–21, 25; iStockphoto, 11, 17, 29; Rolf Vennenbernd/picture-alliance/dpa/AP Images, 12; Photo12/ Ann Ronan Picture Library/Alamy, 14; Jack Vartoogian/Archive Photos/Getty Images, 18; John Everett/ Houston Chronicle/AP Images, 22; Ryan Kang/AP Images, 26

Library of Congress Cataloging-in-Publication Data
Names: Argentine, Cynthia, 1966- author.
Title: Latin music / by Cynthia Argentine.
Description: Mendota Heights, MN: Focus Readers, 2025. | Series: Music genres | Includes index. | Audience: Grades 2-3
Identifiers: LCCN 2024003255 (print) | LCCN 2024003256 (ebook) | ISBN 9798889982036 (hardcover) | ISBN 9798889982593 (paperback) | ISBN 9798889983675 (pdf) | ISBN 9798889983156 (ebook)
Subjects: LCSH: Popular music--Latin America--History and criticism--Juvenile literature.
Classification: LCC ML3475 .A74 2025 (print) | LCC ML3475 (ebook) | DDC 780.98--dc23/eng/20240123
LC record available at https://lccn.loc.gov/2024003255
LC ebook record available at https://lccn.loc.gov/2024003256

Printed in the United States of America
Mankato, MN
082024

About the Author

Cynthia Argentine loves music! She is a piano teacher as well as a writer. Her favorite thing about Latin music is the feel and complexity of its syncopated rhythms. Cynthia enjoys writing about many topics, including music, science, and nature. *Night Becomes Day: Changes in Nature* is one of her award-winning titles.

Table of Contents

Chapter 1

A Live Latin Concert

Crowds fill the streets of a big city. One road is blocked off. A huge stage is set up there. People gather around it. They are excited. The outdoor concert is about to begin.

People often celebrate Latin music and culture at street parties, parades, and music festivals.

On stage, guitar players lift their instruments. The bass guitar player gets ready. Brass players grab trumpets and trombones. Drummers hold their sticks. Then a singer steps up to the mic.

From the first note, the music soars. The horns blast. Drums beat.

Some Latin music concerts happen in stadiums or arenas. Others happen in concert halls or on the street.

Musicians listen to one another as they play. They stay on beat together.

Guitars hum. Spanish lyrics fill the air. The singer steps and claps as he sings. Energy pulses through the crowd. The music makes people dance.

Chapter 2

What Is Latin Music?

Latin music comes from Latin America. More than 30 countries make up this region. It includes Mexico, Central America, and South America. It also includes islands in the Caribbean.

Mariachi is a type of Mexican folk music. Mariachi bands have brass and stringed instruments.

Each area has its own musical traditions. As a result, Latin music involves a wide range of sounds. But the **genre** has some common features. Latin music is usually sung in Spanish or Portuguese. Guitar, trumpet, and accordion are common instruments.

Percussion is another key part of Latin music. Drums and claves often drive the music's beat. Maracas or other shakers add layers to the music's sound.

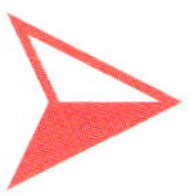

Claves are wooden sticks. They make a clacking sound when hit together.

Latin music is also known for its **rhythms**. The music often accents the **offbeats**. This creates a good rhythm for movement. Artists often hope their audience will dance.

Rumba is a dance style from Cuba. Dancers step back and forth and sway their hips.

Many famous dance styles come from Latin music. For example, the tango was created in Argentina and Uruguay. Tango dancers follow the song's beats with smooth and sharp moves. Samba developed in Brazil. The dance uses fast beats with many patterns. Mambo is another famous Latin dance. It comes from Cuba. Music for mambo dancing includes conga drums. The drums, bass, and cowbell carry the beat.

Brazil's Carnaval is one of the biggest parties in the world. The parades and events are full of Latin music and dance.

Chapter 3

History of Latin Music

Latin music has roots in Latin American history. Hundreds of years ago, the Inca and Aztecs lived in the region. In the late 1400s, Spanish explorers arrived. They brought **enslaved** Africans.

Making music helped enslaved people keep some traditions from their home.

All of these groups made music. Each sound was different. Over hundreds of years, the sounds mixed. For example, some people played Spanish guitar. Then they added **Indigenous** maracas. And African traditional beats drove the tune. These blends became Latin music.

In the 1930s and 1940s, the style developed even further. Cuba was a hot spot. So was Puerto Rico. In these places, Spanish lyrics mixed

In the 1900s, New York City became a center for spreading Latin music and culture.

with African beats. The music gained large audiences.

After that, Latin music spread to new places. Latin Americans moved to the United States. They brought their music with them. Many sounds mixed together again.

Celia Cruz was known as the Queen of Salsa. Salsa mixes musical styles from several countries.

Big bands started using Cuban beats. Latin music met jazz. People loved the new sounds. Artists such as Machito and Tito Puente became popular.

Latin music also mixed with rock. In 1958, Ritchie Valens sang “La

Bamba." It topped the charts. And Carlos Santana's 1970 version of "Oye Como Va" became a classic.

By the 1990s, more and more people had heard Latin music. The style had fans all over Latin America and the United States.

Did You Know?

"Feliz Navidad" is a Latin Christmas song. It was released in Puerto Rico in 1970. Later, it became a major hit on the US charts.

ARTIST SPOTLIGHT

Gloria Estefan

Gloria Estefan was born in Cuba in 1957. She grew up in Miami, Florida. Estefan loved to sing. Music became her career.

In the 1970s, Estefan joined Miami Sound Machine. "Conga" from 1985 became the band's first US hit. The lyrics were in English. But the beats came from Cuban music. Listeners loved it.

Later, Estefan started a **solo** career. She helped take Latin music around the world. By 2024, she had won eight Grammy Awards.

Gloria Estefan sings salsa music, ballads, and pop songs.

Chapter 4

Latin Music Today

In the 1990s, several Latin singers reached superstar status around the world. In 1995, Selena released *Dreaming of You*. The album hit No. 1 in the United States. Selena became a huge star.

In the 1990s, Selena helped spread Latin music around the world.

In 1999, Ricky Martin sang "The Cup of Life" at an awards show. His career exploded. In the 2000s, Shakira captured fans around the world. Marc Anthony and Enrique Iglesias sold millions of albums. Latin music also got its own awards show, the Latin Grammys.

The genre's sound changed over time. Artists created new styles. One modern style is reggaeton. Reggaeton blends Latin with hip-hop and dancehall. Another

Singers such as J Balvin helped sales of Latin music top $1 billion in 2022.

style is merengue. Merengue is a type of fast dance music.

In 2017, Latin music reached a new height of popularity. A song called "Despacito" was released.

In 2020, the Super Bowl halftime show featured Latin music. Shakira (left) and Jennifer Lopez performed.

Latin artists Luis Fonsi and Daddy Yankee made the song. Justin Bieber joined a **remix**. It became the most popular song in the world.

By the 2020s, Latin music was even more mainstream. Artists such as Bad Bunny had some of the biggest hits in the world. Bad Bunny's music is often Latin **trap**. And young artists such as Iván Cornejo often blended styles. Latin music continued to grow.

Lin-Manuel Miranda often uses Latin music in musicals. The 2021 movie *Encanto* is one example. Its song "We Don't Talk About Bruno" topped charts.

FOCUS ON

Latin Music

Write your answers on a separate piece of paper.

1. Write a few sentences explaining some common features of Latin music.

2. Which Latin performer do you think is the best of all time? Why?

3. When did the song "La Bamba" first come out?

- **A.** 1958
- **B.** 1970
- **C.** 1995

4. How did the Justin Bieber remix of "Despacito" help the song spread?

- **A.** All Latin music fans disliked the remix.
- **B.** More fans of different genres heard the song.
- **C.** People only listened to Bieber's part.

5. What does **blends** mean in this book?

One modern style is reggaeton. Reggaeton ***blends*** *Latin with hip-hop and dancehall.*

- **A.** does not like
- **B.** does not use
- **C.** mixes things together

6. What does **mainstream** mean in this book?

By the 2020s, Latin music was even more ***mainstream****. Artists such as Bad Bunny had some of the biggest hits in the world.*

- **A.** less common
- **B.** barely known
- **C.** widely popular

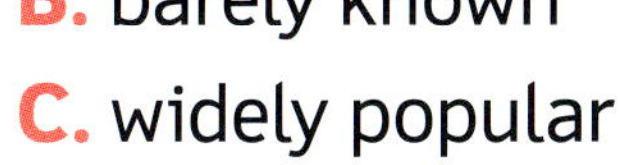

Answer key on page 32.

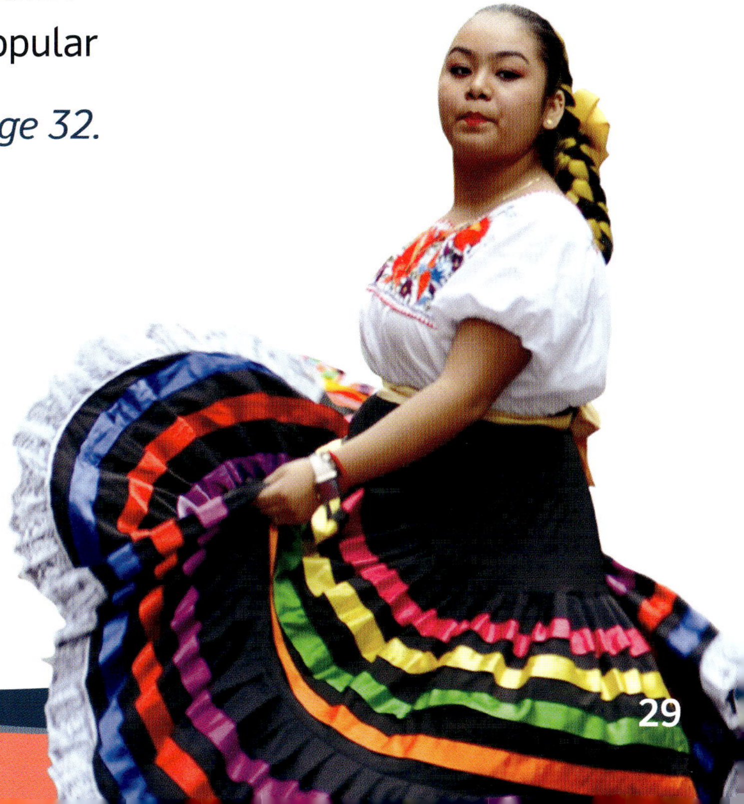

Glossary

enslaved
Forced to work without pay and owned as property.

genre
A style of music.

Indigenous
Related to the native people who lived in a region before colonists arrived.

offbeats
The beats that are often weaker or less emphasized in a piece of music.

percussion
Instruments played by being hit or shaken, such as drums or bells.

remix
A new version of a song with some differences.

rhythms
In music, the mixes of short and long sounds that create patterns.

solo
Done alone rather than with a group.

trap
A style of hip-hop from the southern United States known for its strong percussion.

To Learn More

BOOKS

Abdo, Kenny. *Latin Music History*. Minneapolis: Abdo Publishing, 2020.

Laughlin, Kara L. *Guitars*. Mankato, MN: The Child's World, 2020.

Rossiter, Brienna. *Great Careers in Music*. Mendota Heights, MN: Focus Readers, 2022.

NOTE TO EDUCATORS

Visit **www.focusreaders.com** to find lesson plans, activities, links, and other resources related to this title.

Index

Answer Key: 1. Answers will vary; **2.** Answers will vary; **3.** A; **4.** B; **5.** C; **6.** C